With Love
To Daniel
from Grandma
Christmas 1986

THE
RELUCTANT POTE

To Cher

British Library Cataloguing in Publication Data

Hull, Rod
   The reluctant pote.
  , I. Title   PR6058.U/
   821'.914

     ISBN 0-340-34333-8 (cased)
     ISBN 0-340-36127-1 (paperback)

First published 1983 (cased)
Second impression 1983
First published 1984 (paperback)

Published by Hodder and Stoughton Children's Books,
a division of Hodder and Stoughton Ltd, Mill Road,
Dunton Green, Sevenoaks, Kent TN13 2YJ

Printed in Great Britain by St. Edmundsbury Press,
Bury St. Edmunds, Suffolk. Photoset by
Rowland Phototypesetting (London) Ltd

THE RELUCTANT POTE

ROD HULL

With decorations by Sally Gregory

HODDER AND STOUGHTON
LONDON SYDNEY AUCKLAND TORONTO

CONTENTS

MISS RIX

Miss Rix,
Has a watch that ticks,
A door that sticks,
And a house of bricks.
Summer frocks,
A clock that tocks,
And more than twenty pairs of socks.

In the house of bricks,
With the watch that ticks,
The door that sticks,
And not forgetting poor Miss Rix,
Were seven tiny day-old chicks . . .

In a cardboard box,
'Neath the clock that tocks,
Near a cupboard full of summer frocks
(Not to mention all those socks).

The chicks went 'cheep'
In tones quite deep,
That woke Miss Rix from her morning sleep
And stopped the clock,
(The one that tocks),
And gave Miss Rix several minor shocks.

'You naughty chicks,'
Said the shocked Miss Rix,
'I'll search throughout this house of bricks
To find some locks
For your cardboard box.'
(She found them too – underneath the socks).

Now the day-old chicks
Play no more tricks
In the house of bricks,
With the watch that ticks,

The clock that tocks,
The frocks and socks.
But the door still sticks,
Poor Miss Rix.

WHEN I BECOME PRIME MINISTER

When I become Prime Minister,
Well . . . just you wait an' see.
We won't have any money
'Cos ev'rythin' will be free.
Like sweets an' toys an' cakes an' things,
An' circuses an' zoos,
An' just cartoons on the telly,
An' no more silly News.

An' lots of things will be allowed,
Like balancing cups on your head,
An' standing near the stove when it's hot,
An' jumping on the bed.
An' riding your bike in the street when you like,
An' camp fires on the lawn,
An' it'll be ''gainst-the-law' to moan at folks
What jes' get their trousers torn.

An' all the cabbages in the land
We'll send abroad to sell,
An' people what *actually like* 'em . . .
Well . . . they can go as well.

I 'spec we'll have to keep the schools
Jes' so's we can learn,
But when we queue up for the swings
We *all* will get a turn.

An' balloons will be on every street
For 'pensh'ners' an' folks like them.
I bet people jus' can't wait
'Til I become P.M.

MISS BLEEP

Old man Buzz and dear Miss Bleep
Live in my telephone.
I pick it up and listen
To see if they're at home.
It's always grumpy Mr Buzz
Who sounds like he's asleep,
So I just dial a number
And listen to Miss Bleep.
One day I dialled a lot of them
And heard a strange 'burr-burr',
I didn't like the sound of him
(Or perhaps it was a her).
But today I found out something,
Mr Buzz can't be so aged,
For an operator told me
Miss Bleep had become engaged.

POTTERS BAR

To be sung in harmony by three
unaccompanied male voices.

Hurrah! Hurrah!
To be in Potters Bar!
People travel near and far,
By boat and train and bus and car,
So bring your Ma and bring your Pa,
And come to Potters Bar!

Hurrah! Hurrah!
To be in Potters Bar!
Set your course by Stellar Maris,
It takes you to where Potters Bar is,
In some arcade with a Potters Barmaid,
We'll drink to Potters Bar!

Hurrah! Hurrah!
People from afar,
From Chester and from Derby, you
Join in a Potters Barbecue.
All the rest of the world are rotters!
In every place, that is,
Bar Potters!

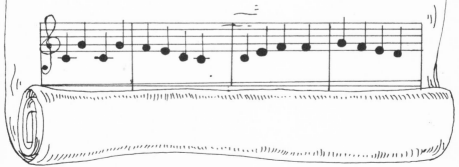

15

THE FISH

Arnold Pish caught a fish
In a brightly coloured net.
He stuffed it in his pocket
To keep it as a pet.

He put it in a special nest,
A flower pot lined with straw,
And fed it crumpets, once a week,
Which he rolled across the floor.

Arnold Pish taught his fish
How to climb a tree,
What to do to mend a fuse,
And warm the pot for tea.

16

Every night at six o'clock,
Except when it was dark,
The two would jog for seven miles
Round and round the park.

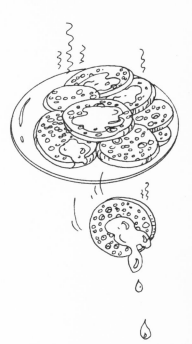

They'd walk the hills and run the downs
And rest upon the ridge,
And then they'd race each other home
Across the narrow bridge.

One night the bridge was slippery,
Arnold heard a sound.
Too late! The poor fish slipped and fell
. . . in the river and was drowned!

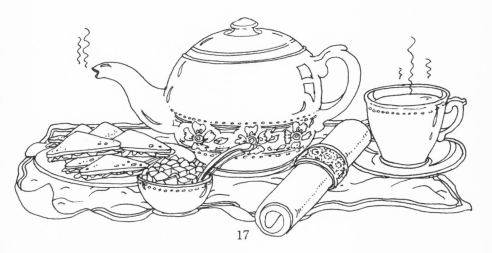

NOT AN ORIGINAL POME
For people what can't rite their own pomes.

Not a drum was heard, not a funeral note,
But his Captain's hand on his shoulder smote,
The fair breeze blew, the white foam flew,
'Good speed!' cried the watch, as the gate-bolts undrew.

And all I ask is a tall ship
And a star to steer her by,
Laces for a lady,
Letters for a spy,
Great rats, small rats, black rats, grey,
Firewood, ironware, and cheap tin trays.

THE BULLY

'Where do you live?' the bully said,
'I'll not tell you,' said I,
'Tell me or I'll bash you up,'
But I did not reply.
He advanced on me, his fist upraised.
I stood firmly on my feet.
Then he punched me on the nose,
So I said '23, Albert Street.'

HANDS

Tiny fingers grasping, just
One of yours, in hope and trust.
Being led along the way
Until, a few short years away,
Small hand grips that of another,
Guides, protects, a baby brother.
Through feeble hand of spotted youth,
Brushing aside in search of truth,
To firmer hand that holds one fair
And promises to love and share.
Then family hand no longer broods,
Savours life in all its moods.
Hands in friendship, clenched aggression,
Hands that give and take possession,
Hands that play,
Hands that toil,
Hands that shape,
Hands that spoil.
Rich hands, poor hands, hands that pray,
Hands well met along life's way.
Skilled hands, wise hands,
Hands that care and tend,
Weathered hand, older hand,
Until, towards the end,
The lesson learnt of life reveals
The joy of duty, as your hand feels
Tiny fingers grasping, just
One of yours, in hope and trust.

FOUR LITTLE GNOMES FROM THE LAND OF KRID

Four little gnomes from the land of Krid
One named Gumpy, another one, Zid.
One called Took-shoe, the fourth one Hurn,
Were told to leave and not return.

For Hurn is the gnome who comes in the night
And taps on your window to give you a fright,

Zid is the one who *makes* you tell lies
So that Father stares with suspicion in his eyes,

And when Mother says 'Do
Try and find your other shoe,'
You can guess which gnome
Has been to visit you,

And when no-one believes your innocent blink,
It was Gumpy who made you spill your drink.

Four little gnomes from the Land of Krid,
Gumpy, Took-shoe, Hurn and Zid.
No wonder they were banished
For the things they did.

THE CANNIBALS

My father and I stayed with cannibals.
We played golf with them through the rough gorse,
And when we returned we had dinner,
Except Dad,
Who was the Pa for the course.

MARCH DAY

It's a wet and windy day outside
When cat lies sleeping by the fire,
And watery pearls are whipped away
From hedgerows dripping briar.

And dark grey curtain of stormy sky
Quiets all its drenched domain,
Save chirping blackbirds as they dart
Through crocus cupped with rain.

And cold wet stone of village church
Drips history to the ground,
Upon the glistening church path flags
Each drop, soaked up, unfound.

Not so in town, where pavements wet
Reflect the bustling feet,
With sploshes, galoshes and dripping mackintoshes
Dried out by gas-fire's heat.

Nor so the stormy seaside fronts
Where waves invade the prom,
And a lonely rain-soaked awning flaps
And longs for days to come.

In town and country, all the land
Is dressed in wet attire.
A cold and windy wet March day
And cat lies sleeping by the fire.

MY PRINTING SET HAS LOST ITS 'E'

I HAD A PRINTING S*T FOR CHRISTMAS,
I WAS HAPPY AS COULD B*.
I PRINT*D LOTS AND LOTS OF THINGS,
UNTIL I LOST TH* '*'.

OF ALL THR LYTTYRS IN THK ALPHABWT,
THU ONT I HAVD TO LOSQ
HAS TO BH THJ FIFTH ONZ,
THL ONG MOST COMMONLY USBD.

SO NOW WHTN I DO PRINTING,
XACH TIMK I COMV TO '*',
I US* ANOTHIR LOTTUR,
THAT'S HOW IT HAS TO BN.

26

A SORT OF RIDDLE

My first is in Terrapins but not in Transpire.
My second's in Reside but not in Desire.
My third is in Stainer but not in Retains.
My fourth is in Sanction but not in Contains.
My last is in Loaf but not in Foal.
Search through 'A RAGMANS' and you'll find my whole.

CLEANING LADIES

Eve and Sue are ladies who
Will come and clean the house for you.
They arrive at ten and leave at two
And then they hurry home.

With dusters, buckets, mops and brooms,
They rush around and clean the rooms,
And fill the vases with new blooms,
Before they hurry home.

Wherever Eve and Sue have been,
The place is always bright and clean.
But when they're done, it seems they're keen
To always hurry home.

They always say my room's the worst,
And 'looks as if a bomb has burst'.
They know if they don't do it first,
They'll never hurry home.

If I lose a toy, it's back next day,
And all my books are packed away.
If only Eve and Sue could stay
And never hurry home.

A FUNNY POME

If every gnu, in London Zoo,
Disappeared forever,
You'd have to say, 'That's the end of the gnus –
– And now it's time for the weather.'

THE GARDEN CENTRE

The Garden Centre's a special sort of place,
It's all laid out in lots of space.
There's clematis, and fizzy drinks,
And forget-me-nots as well,
And chocolate bars, and foxgloves.
They've lots of things to sell,
Like pansies, and ice-creams,
And things called 'will-o-wisps',
Lemonade, and marigolds, and cheese and onion crisps.
And if you're feeling tired,
You can try the garden swings,
Or lay down in a summer house,
They've lots and lots of things.
My father likes to take me,
(He says I've something called a flair),
I've only been there once,
But I know everything that's there.

FOUR LITTLE GNOMES FROM THE LAND OF KRID *A Sequel*

Four little gnomes from the Land of Krid,
Gumpy, Took-shoe, Hurn and Zid,
(The ones who were banished for the things they did)
Laughed as beneath a snowdrop hid.

But the four were in for a big surprise,
The snowdrop . . . was a fairy! (in disguise),
She turned and raised her arms to the skies
And stared at them all with angry eyes.

'You naughty little gnomes,' cried the snowdrop queen,
'You've got children into trouble wherever you've been.'

'Bah!' said Gumpy, 'don't *you* start.'
'No,' said Took-shoe, 'we're really smart.'
'Boo!' said Zid and Hurn said 'Pish!
If you're a fairy grant us a wish!'
'Make us statues!'
'So people can inspect –'
'– Us poor maligned creatures,'
'And treat us with respect!'

'Oh', said the fairy, 'do you think I should?
Perhaps I will! . . . I'll make you good!'
The world, she thought, would soon concur
What well-behaved, sweet-natured gnomes they
                                        were.

So she waved her wand
(To make the transition)
And they became the Ideal Gnomes Exhibition.

THE LAMB IN SPRING

See the little lamb in spring,
He jumps and skips and hops.
And gambols through the fields so green,
With jumps and skips and hops.
He dances up the village street,
All jumps and skips and hops,
Whoops! he's in the butcher's,
Jumps and skips and chops!

LAST WILL AND TESTAMENT

This is . . . .

The last will and testament
Of poor old Bill (in a vest he went).
Died while picnicking in the woods.
Left behind no worldly goods.

In his last will and testament.

Nil for Jill (the wife he sent)
From their soirée in the glade
To summon ambulance and first aid.
Urging on her quest be bent
(Requesting only the best be sent)
Hurrying, speeding to get there fast,
To the spot where Bill had coughed his last.

Will and testament,
Poor old Bill, to his rest he went.
Help arrived just minutes late,
To find words scrawled on paper plate,
'I think perhaps in the best event,
I'll leave no will – just testament.'

IN BED

When I'm in bed and Mummy sings,
It makes me think of lovely things.
All that happened when we went to play.
We chased a rabbit, but he got away.
I climbed a tree and we went on the swings.
It's lovely to think when Mummy sings.

When Mummy sings,
When I'm in bed,
My eyes go a bit heavy,
And so does my head.
But I'll think of some more,
If I lay on my tummy . . .
No . . . I'll lay on my side,
And just listen to Mummy.

The more and more that Mummy sings
Makes it harder to think of things.
Oh, I remember this morning – the fun we had!
We hid under the table – and frightened Dad!

I had a quick yawn then,
Don't believe Mummy saw,
But I really don't think
I can think any more.

It's a pretty song that Mummy sings,
But it makes it hard to think of things.
The bed's nice and warm and I sink down all deep.
Oh, that song Mummy sings
Always . . .
Sends . . .
Me . . .
To . . .
. . . .

A POME ABOUT MY DAD

Dad was never much good at gardening,
His plants were all stunted and small.
Each year he would sow as much as he could,
Hardly anything came up at all.

Retired now, he's taken up Bonsai,
It's gentle and he can't make a goof.
He says he is pleased – 'It's quite a success,
They're growing up right through the roof!'

ON SEEING A HULK OF A SHIP
DECAYING IN MILTON CREEK

Great seas once spilled o'er your solid decks,
Now broken twigs and dead leaves lay.
Stout sides that rode white horse's necks,
Quiet waters lap and ducks do play.
Mighty helm with rain lashed hands,
Steered ocean-wide to distant lands,
Now all you view, a narrow creek,
Tied to green banks less adventures you seek,
A tree your companion, new in spring bud
While planks from your side fall to rot in the mud.

39

THOUGHTS OF A LITTLE BOY LOOKING OUT
OF HIS BEDROOM WINDOW

I'll not go out to play to-day,
There's a tiger loose outside.
I saw him from my bedroom
Go behind a bush and hide.

There's something else I know of,
. . . a giant in the shed!
The kind that grabs you suddenly
And grinds your bones for bread.

There's lions in the greenhouse
And bears down by the gate,
And monsters hiding in the trees
And wolves that lie in wait.

And witches dancing on the lawn
With bats and toads and weasels.
No, I think I'll stay in bed to-day,
I have to, I've got measles!

JOAN AND JOYCE

Joan and Joyce toiled all the week,
Serving tea in the rush hour peak.
Rolls and pies from the Breakfast Bar,
At the station buffet for B.R.

From six to nine was all non-stop,
Then once round quickly with the mop,
Then a quiet sit down, but as Joan said,
'After half past nine, this place is dead.'

'I know we're rushed and we both complain,
But I miss them when they board their train.
We must do something to make them stay –
To-morrow we'll give them . . . CABARET!'

Next day dawned with the factory hooters,
The place was jam-packed with commuters,
When from behind the Breakfast Bar
Came the twanging of Joan's guitar.

Passengers' faces lit up smiles,
As she danced across the tea-stained tiles.
Then came Joyce with yet more tunes
(She played 'Granada' on the spoons).

More tea followed, rolls and cokes,
'Companied by Joan telling jokes,
Toast and coffee, the place was packed,
While Joyce performed her conjuring act.

No-one got to work that day,
They stayed to watch the cabaret.
You couldn't get through the restaurant doors,
While the buffet rocked to wild applause.

Now, with takings up by half,
The station's taken on more staff.
British Rail, they wanted more,
So Joan and Joyce have gone on tour.

At station buffets through the land,
Commuters give them such a hand.
Try to catch them if you're able.
That's if you can book a table.

AN ENGLISH POME

The sun shone from a cloudless sky
O'er England's fields of corn,
And dried each poppy's dew-dropped eye
To greet the summer's morn.

A far off skylark's joyful song,
The great oak's dappled leaves,
The scent of summer borne along
By gentle warming breeze.

The trickling of the sleepy brook,
The lush green sward – so thick,
And all around – sweet heavenly peace . . .
Doesn't it make you sick?

FIRST DAY AT SCHOOL

My first day at school to-day.
Funny sort of day.
Didn't seem to learn much.
Seemed all we did was play.
Then teacher wrote some letters
On a board all painted black,
And then we had a story and . . .
I don't think I'll go back.

HIM TO A HOMONYM

They grieved for him that early mourn,
And through the misty rain,
Even the vintners began to wine,
And the weathercock looked vane.

They all formed up and stood in tiers,
The painted bells were peeling.
The laundress wept and rung her hands,
Her perfume scent one reeling.

The large fat lady took big size.
She thought it was a waist,
She knew him as a fugitive,
Though he was always chaste.

'Twas in Italy he began to rome,
And went from town to town,
Posing as a preacher,
Until he was tract down.
The courtroom heard a plaintiff sound.
No-one could have dreamed,
The travelling tramp was a Scholar of Rhodes,
And well tailored, so it seamed.

The jury retired to consider.
All were ill at ease.
Even the children in school were taut,
While the tormentors had their tease.

It was the hangman who broke the noose in the end,
News nobody wanted to hear.
In their uniforms they serged forward,
To the pub where the corpse had a bier.

All went away – but the sober staid,
And the bootmender, he sold his shoes.
And with the carpenter who gave his awl,
They became seamen and went on a crews.

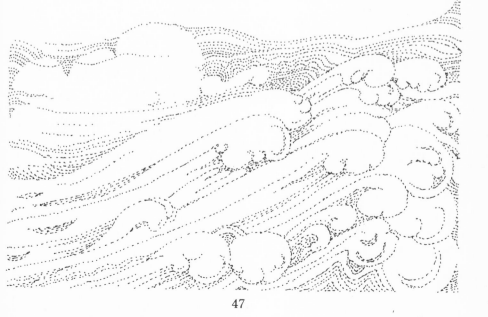

THE DIFFERENCE

Sometimes, at night, when I sit by your bed
And look at you, son – your sleeping young head –
I think of the difference between me and you.
The fields where you play, I used to play too.
And where you lie back and stare at the sky,
I did the same, but I saw people die.

My sky was full of bullets and planes,
A 'dogfight' they called it – such strange, adult games.
You play on the beach and run 'til you tire,
That same beach for me was meshed with barbed wire.
You collect conkers that fall in the road,
I picked up shrapnel – made to explode.

Sirens and blackouts and evacuation,
Gas-masked and labelled and sent to the station,
Forcing on shoes that had to make do,
Clothing that lasted until it wore through.
Few sweets, little food, no comics nor toys,
The shelters each night lest we were destroyed.
Sardine-packed in damp, musty bed,
While corrugated canopy dripped overhead.

I was happy in my way, it was all that I knew.
I'm glad, dear son, that it's different for you.
When you call in the night, you know I am here,
I never saw my dad for many a year.

Don't heed my thoughts for yesterday's strife.
Sleep on in peace for the rest of your life.

AN OLD SOAK'S SONG

I'm not well and I haven't been well since 1924.
The doctor said when he saw me stagger
Through his surgery door,
'You need brandy,
Keep some handy,
Drink it every day
And if you do you won't get the 'flu –
That's all I have to say.'

I.O.U.

Bill's a good mate,
A true and trusted friend.
He's not exactly tight, is Bill,
But he's not inclined to spend.

He'd always help a mate out,
Especially one like me.
Why, I remember just last year
He lent me 50p.

He's not let me forget it though,
He's the kind that frets,
And the conversation always turns
To people paying debts.

Things got to a head last week,
He wants an I.O.U!
Written on a paper and
Signed and witnessed too!

So this little rhyme is just for him,
If he kindly will
Accept this verse I've written,
As an owed to Bill.

OPPOSITES

Opposite to go is stop.
Opposite to skip is hop.
Opposite to up is down.
Opposite to smile is frown.

Opposite to good is bad.
Opposite to happy, sad.
Opposite to 'Sshhh' is *SHOUT*!
Opposite to in is out.

Opposite to run is walk.
Opposite to sing is talk.

There are so many opposites under the sun,
And Mummy says I'm every one!

That means,
I sing and talk and run and walk,
I 'sshhh' and shout, I'm in, I'm out,
I'm happy, sad and good and bad,
I smile, I frown, I'm up, I'm down,
I skip and hop and go and . . . stop!

The opposite to play is rest
And the one I think that mum likes best,
When in my room she takes a peep
At the opposite me . . . asleep!

A cross between a sonnet full of puns and a Tom Swiftie is called a Swiftie Punnet. This one is entitled . . .

SLOW-LEA O'ER THE -LY

'My pulse is racing much too fast,'
She said, wholeheartedly.
'That's 'cos you don't play cricket,'
He answered, headingly.
'I'd rather take my clothes off,'
She said, gypsyroselee.
'Oh dear, that's made me feel quite faint,'
He sighed, salvolatile.

POST OFFICE VANS

All the Post Office vans that you see,
Painted red,
Have all been painted by a man called Fred.
Fred was a proud and very happy man
When the Post Office gave him a brand new van.
'It's all yours, Fred,' the foreman would say,
'Paint it red, have it finished by to-day.'
A brand new van was a challenge to Fred
And by the end of the day it would be bright red.

But one day Fred thought he's try something new,
So he asked the foreman what he thought of blue.
'Dear me, no . . . That wouldn't do, Fred,
Post Office vans are always red.'
But the foreman said that Fred should decide
On special words to write on the side.

Fred thought for a while and bit his nail,
Said, 'What if I write – er, – Royal Mail?'
'Excellent thought,' the foreman cried.
And 'ER ROYAL MAIL' is on the side
Of every Post Office van in sight.
Look for yourself, you'll see I'm right.

MORE THOUGHTS FROM A LITTLE BOY

'No tuck for Toby on Friday,
If he has a moan and a cry day.'
That's what they normally say as a rule,
When I'm sent upstairs to get ready for school.

When you've just started school,
It's a bit of a cheek
To want you to behave
Every day of the week.
I've lost one of my shoes
And I can't find my tie.
'Sno wonder I have a bit of a cry.
I could nip down the stairs,
Grab my coat and my cap and. . .
Walk out of the house as if nothing has happened!
They might not notice
And, with any luck,
They'll give me my money – so I can buy tuck!
Oh, there's Mum on the stairs...
I'll never get by.
Oh goody! She's found my shoe and my tie.
'Now come along, Toby, and let's get you dressed.
We want you to leave home looking your best.
And because you've been helpful and quiet when you play,
Here's 10p to spend as it's tuck day to-day.'

I don't think I'll spend it.
Well, perhaps I'll spend some,
But I'll save all the rest, and buy something for Mum.

A VERY, VERY OLDE POME
What Could Have Been Rit in Shakespeare's Time

Oh mistress mine for meat I crave,
Hey Nonny Nonny Noh,
Pray cook me some in thy microwave,
Hey Nonny Nonny Noh.
For Summer is a-coming in,
Bang your drum or plastic bin,
Oh prithee plight yon damsel's troth,
Who dress doth look like an old J-cloth,
Hey Nonny Nonny Noh . . . Oh.

KISSES

I don't like kissing Grandad,
He always seems so prickly,
And I don't like kissing babies much,
They're always wet and sickly.
And I don't like kissing aunties
Who've got powder on their cheek,
And I really hate those people
Who kiss you as you speak.
I don't like kissing uncles,
'Cos they always smell of beer.
I don't mind people who've got colds
'Cos they say, 'Don't come near.'
Daddy always smells of smoke,
But he's better than the rest.
But of all the people in the world,
I like kissing Mummy best.
Sometimes when she's kissed me,
I lick it all away,
Then swallow it and keep it
To have another day.

RONALD/DONALD

Ronald Derds (or was it Donald Rerds?)
Was a boy who always wixed up his merds.
If anyone asked him; 'What's the time?'
He'd look at his watch and say, 'Norter past quine.'

He's spoken like that ever since he was two.
His parents at first didn't know what to do.
In order to understand what he'd said,
His father would get him to stand on his head.

But this didn't work, something had to be done,
So Ma and Pa Derds learnt to speak like their son.

'Mood gorning,' he'd cry, as he chat in his sair.
'Gorning,' they'd answer, without hurning a tair.
And Ron's Mum would say, 'Get a nice brofe of led,'
For Ron to return with a loaf of fresh bread.

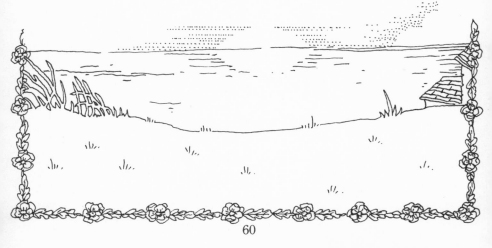

Then one special day, young Ronald's voice broke.
He found it affected the way that he spoke.
'Good morning,' he said as he sat in his chair.
'Gorning,' said the others and started to stare.

From that moment on, things just got worse.
The harder they tried, they just couldn't converse.

Ron said to his parents, after a week,
'It's driving me mad, the way that you speak.
I can't understand a word that you say.
You leave me no option, I'm leaving to-day.'

So Ron joined the Navy and sailed to the Barents,
To get as far away as he could from his parents.
And although this story all seems rather sad,
Ron occasionally visits his Dum and his Mad.